Photography by Richard Bennett

Text by Bruce Montgomery

Published and distributed by Richard Bennett
PO Box 385, Kingston, Tasmania 7051
Telephone: +61 3 6229 2559

Facsimile: +61 3 6229 7725
email: richard@richardbennett.com.au
www.richardbennett.com.au

First published in Australia 2004 by Richard Bennett
Photographs Copyright Richard Bennett 2004

Graphics by de Vos design
Photographed on Fujifilm
Scanning by Photolith
Printing by the Printing Authority of Tasmania

ISBN 0-9578110-2-0

Every effort has been made to ensure that the information in this book is accurate at the time
of going to press. The publisher cannot accept responsibility for any errors or omissions.

TASMANIA
THE WILD ISLAND

RICHARD BENNETT

Cockscomb Ridge, Mt La Perouse

FOREWORD

Sir Guy Green – Former Governor of Tasmania

Comprising an archipelago of one large island and 343 smaller ones that extend from the sub-Antarctic to the mainland of Australia, Tasmania is a truly remarkable place with an extensive network of mighty rivers and sparkling streams, thousands of lakes, wild rocky coastlines, hundreds of kilometres of glorious beaches, magnificent mountains and alpine plateaux, huge tracts of rainforest and wilderness, productive agricultural lands, modern cities, lovely villages, superb harbours and waterways, a greater stock of listed Georgian and Victorian buildings than the rest of Australia put together, a benign maritime temperate climate and enveloped by a crystal clear atmosphere with a glowing luminosity that has inspired some of the finest landscape painters in the world.

Nurtured, shaped and inspired by its environment, Tasmania is just as remarkable as a society as it is as a place. Its decentralised population comprises many strong, proud communities that are rich in social capital and imbued with the ethos of volunteerism. Tasmanians, like other island dwellers, have a strong sense of identity and a broad outward-looking perspective on the rest of Australia and the world. Tasmania has an impressive 200-year history of creativity, innovation and excellence in the arts, law, science, technology and social development. Today it is also known internationally for its fine foods and beverages, as a tourist destination and in many other fields ranging from marine science, agriculture and aquaculture through to shipbuilding, education, Antarctic affairs, yacht racing and renewable energy production.

In recent years Tasmania has also witnessed an exciting renaissance in craft and design, music and the performing and visual arts and the advent of highly successful arts festivals.

This fine work makes a significant addition to renowned Tasmanian photographer Richard Bennett's other impressive publications. The pictures reflect the extraordinary character of the Tasmanian environment: its complexity, mystery and freshness, the sharpness and clarity of its atmosphere and the subtlety, variety and richness of the colours of its vegetation, landscapes and seascapes. The photographs are so vivid as to appear almost unreal but in fact visitors find that the reality is even more striking.

Augmented by fascinating essays on Tasmania's geological platform, its ancient origins in Gondwana and the interaction between its people and the environment, this book is a wonderful evocation of a very special part of the world.

Cockscomb Ridge, Mt La Perouse

TASMANIA IS THE WAY IT IS because of its geological history. Its location, its wildlife and vegetation, its landforms, its attractions, our way of life are all controlled by the past!

We know that 80 per cent of earth's history had passed before the earliest known history of Tasmania began. At this time – about 800 million years ago – there were no animals, no plants on land, no soil and Tasmania was in the northern hemisphere! It was a totally different world. Tasmania was part of an amalgamation of continents and continental fragments – Pangaea – that included virtually all the Earth's continents.

Between this time and 550 million years, the main rocks of south-west, west and north-west Tasmania were formed.

At 550 million years, Pangaea split into two, leaving one smaller supercontinent, Gondwana. That event has controlled our history ever since.

The basement of Tasmania, best visible on the west coast and in the South-West Wilderness Area, is complex and not fully understood. It formed when there was no vegetation on the Earth's surface, when erosion and deposition were very active. Rocks formed thick and fast.

These rocks wrap around and lie under the Tasmania Basin in central and south-eastern Tasmania. They control the landforms of south-western Tasmania and contain most of the State's mineral wealth. They include rocks formed in the ocean, by active volcanism and distorted during a series of major earth movements that destroyed much of their original character. Younger rocks contain fossils which help us document their age and the environment at the time of deposition.

The Tasmania Basin provides our strongest links to Antarctica. Rocks here were formed when Australia was alongside Antarctica. They match rocks of the same age in the Transantarctic Mountains. The older rocks of this sequence, sedimentary rocks of Permian age, contain two features responsible for the concept of Gondwana, the leaf fossil Glossopteris and evidence of glaciation. A younger set of rocks, you see their features in the facades of many buildings in Macquarie St, Hobart and Collins St, Melbourne – sediments again, of Triassic age – lacks any evidence of glaciation even though Antarctica was over the South Pole at the time. Polar ice-sheets are rare in the geological record!

The major rock of significance in Tasmania is the Jurassic dolerite. You see it on the top of Mt Wellington, Cradle Mountain and throughout the Central Plateau. It controls so much of our scenery. It occurs in Tasmania, Kangaroo Island, near Nelson in New Zealand and through the Transantarctic Mountains. It is the truest link we have with the southern continent. In contrast with the other rocks of the Tasmania Basin, it is igneous; it intruded as a hot dry fluid, originating perhaps 100km down in the Earth's crust before rising and spreading out laterally into the pre-existing sedimentary rocks as a series of sheets normally about 350 metres thick and 180-170 million years old. Dolerite is hard and resistant to erosion in this climate.

Thus the framework of modern Tasmania was established, next to Antarctica.

At about 55 million years ago, Australia began moving north from Antarctica at its current rate of about six centimetres per year. By 33.5 million years, it had moved far enough north that ocean waters began circulating around Antarctica, allowing surface waters to cool and for the modern ice-sheet to start, wiping out vegetation and dependent organisms from Antarctica. Until this time, Antarctica had not hosted an ice-sheet since the Permian age.

The vegetation on Antarctica had been essentially that of Tasmania and South America. Now each continent became isolated and evolved in different directions. From the margins of Antarctica we have a record of some vegetation very similar to that now on Tasmania – manferns, southern beech (some almost identical with our deciduous beech), native pepper, guitar plant, sundews, celery-top and Huon pine, creeping pine, Richea. This list can be expected to grow with time and study.

But the separation from Antarctica had other, more obvious consequences! As Tasmania moved north, it underwent tension in a north-east/south-west direction and the crust under the island fractured into a series of raised (horsts) and dropped (graben) blocks. Some examples are the Coal River graben, Derwent graben, Tamar graben and the Macquarie Harbour graben. The graben are where our current rivers flow, the sites of our cities and some of our major tourist attractions. The horsts are our mountains. With this relief and our movement into our current latitude, we enjoy a climate and a precipitation regime that allow us to utilise hydro-electric or wind power.

The fracturing of Tasmania occurred along a series of faults and these were, a little later, the location along which volcanic rocks erupted at the surface, providing us with excellent soils, notably along the north-west coast.

Over the past few million years, while a geologically stable location, Tasmania has experienced the comings and goings of small ice-caps. About 18,000 years ago, there were ice-caps on Mt Field, Cradle Mountain/Lake St Clair (glacial erosion excavated Lake St Clair, Lake Seal and the Broad River Valley), around Queenstown and on the northern parts of the Central Plateau. Our ice-caps and cool intervals occurred at the same time as elsewhere on Earth and coincided with a time of lowered sea level (120 metres lower 18,000 years ago) that allowed migration of plants and animals, including people, across a dry land-bridge through eastern Tasmania, via Flinders Island, to mainland Australia.

This history has controlled the evolution of our modern environment in all its manifestations.

Professor Patrick Quilty

Pigsty Ponds, Mt La Perouse

THE WILD ISLAND

Bruce Montgomery

When you grow up on an island, you may spend your formative years being obsessed with developing plots on how to get off that island.

The surrounding waters become a psychological barrier that imprisons you. You constantly scan the horizon for a glimpse of greener pastures where life must be better, more interesting, more exciting. Life, you sense, is passing you by.

But the island that you regarded as a backwater at this time, takes on a new dimension when you return, having seen the state of the world outside.

Because you seldom, if ever, left this island in those formative years, you never quite appreciated its qualities. In later life, you will learn that those qualities set this island, Tasmania, apart from anywhere else in the world.

The fledgling spreads its wings and explores the distant lands that had promised so much beyond the horizon of the strait, ancient lands that are the cradle of civilisation, yet now worn and despoiled lands, beneath the heavy pallour of a smoky haze that never clears.

When you return to Tasmania, you see this island with new eyes. You see unfiltered images, through the medium of the clearest air in the world, of a pristine place. For there is a hue to Tasmania's light. It is ice blue. It gives our landscapes a clarity and a resolution that you cannot see in Europe or in Asia. Here the colours are sharp and true.

Twenty years ago, the photographer Lord Snowdon described a colour spectrum that had inspired artists Nolan, Boyd and Whiteley. It is that spectrum, he said, enhanced by the natural blue filter of our light that made our landscapes.

Tasmania is an ancient place.

Our forests derive from the supercontinent of Gondwana, a huge landmass that was composed of present-day South America, Africa, Antarctica, India and Australia.

Gondwana began to disintegrate about 160 million years ago. Scientists believe that the Australian continent started to form as a separate entity about 55 million years ago, probably the product of a prolonged series of massive earth movements that dispersed the primeval Gondwanan rainforests.

A consequence was the creation of a passage of sea between Australia and Antarctica, dominated by cold ocean currents. These freeze-dried the Antarctic landmass, making extinct its terrestrial plants and animals. Meanwhile, the Australian continent was transformed from a warm and wet place dominated by rainforest to a largely hot and arid land.

As Australia separated from Antarctica, new plants and animals evolved, the plants dominated by eucalypts and acacias.

The Australian "ark", its plants and animals already derived from both Antarctica and the Australian isolated entity, moved closer to Asia. From there, airborne species and those that drifted south on the sea further diversified our stock.

By the time of European settlement, Australia's rainforests had shrunk to just one per cent of the land surface. They are found today in the mountains and lowlands of the coast, "islands" of rainforest surrounded by classic Australian dry eucalypt forests.

Southport Lagoon

Tasmania's "islands" of rainforest are dominated by species of plants and animals with a clear Gondwanan origin, according to heritage consultant Peter Hitchcock.

"The cool temperate rainforests of the Tasmanian wilderness are probably as close in composition and structure as any forest on the Australian Plate to that of the ancient Gondwanan forests, including those of Antarctica before it went into deep freeze," he says.

"They are dense, dark and cool rainforests, often with only one or two tree species present. Understorey, vines and epiphytic ferns are rare or inconspicuous.

"The dominant tree species, including the myrtle beech (Nothofagus cunninghamii) … reveal their Gondwanan ancestry."

Many of the Tasmanian species have changed little since the time of Gondwana.

There are two altitudes from which to understand the geology of Tasmania – at sea level and from the top of a mountain.

Westerly winds sweep across the Southern Ocean in the mid-southern latitudes known as the Roaring Forties.

Tasmania is an island, but it is also an archipelago of 315 islands. The smallest, like Pedra Branca and Mewstone Rock off the south coast, are as spectacular and significant to the local wildlife as the biggest. Macquarie Island in the sub-Antarctic, 1500 kilometres south-east of the Tasmanian mainland, is our southern outpost.

Just as Tasmania, then named Van Diemen's Land, was originally a penal settlement for the British, the islands of the Furneaux group in north-eastern Tasmania served to isolate Tasmania's Aborigines when they found their solitude invaded.

In the mid-19th century the dwindling numbers of Aborigines who survived the first waves of European settlement were transferred to Flinders Island in the Furneaux group. It was a move that hastened their demise. The settlement at Wybalenna, north of Whitemark, is one of the most significant and haunting historic sites in Tasmania.

King Island, at the western entrance to Bass Strait, is littered with the wrecks of ships driven onto uncharted lee shores. Among them is the Cataraqui, which foundered with the loss of 400 lives, representing Australia's worst ever maritime disaster. The Cataraqui had sailed from Liverpool for Melbourne in April 1845. She had heaved to off the west coast of King Island during a howling gale in August. Shortly after getting underway, she ran aground and huge seas swept her decks and she broke up.

Tasmania's majestic southern capes viewed from the Southern Ocean show this wild island to be a dolerite garrison. The capes are awesome, sheer cliffs rising hundred of metres to protect the hinterland behind them. Viewed from offshore, they superimpose themselves upon each other, framed against the sky in ever-lightening shades of grey, from pure black through to opaque white, eight zones of grey mastered by the American monochrome landscape photographer Ansel Adams.

Stand atop the mountains of the Western Arthurs or Federation Peak and the landscape spreads out before you. This is indeed a special place.

Three months before he drowned in the Gordon River in January 1972 the Tasmanian landscape photographer Olegas Truchanas wrote that Tasmania could become "a shining beacon in a dull, uniform and largely artificial world".

"When we look round, the time is rapidly approaching when the natural environment, natural unspoiled vistas are sadly beginning to look like leftovers from a vanishing world," Truchanas said.

"This vanishing world is beautiful beyond our dreams and contains in itself rewards and gratifications never found in artificial landscape, or man-made objects, so often regarded as exciting evidence of a new world in the making."

Tasmania has more of its land area set aside in national parks and conservation reserves than any other State, 40 per cent.

Five of the parks – the vast South-West National Park, the Franklin-Gordon Wild Rivers National Park, Cradle Mountain-Lake St Clair, the Walls of Jerusalem and Hartz Mountains – constitute the Tasmanian Wilderness World Heritage Area. This status puts it on the same footing with the Taj Mahal, the Egyptian pyramids, the Acropolis, the Serengeti plains in Africa and the Grand Canyon. All are World Heritage properties.

The South-West National Park is Tasmania's largest, an area of high mountains, dense rainforest, button grass plains, wild rivers and an isolated coastline. The south-west draws bushwalkers and climbers from around the world. The two main tracks meet at Port Davey to provide a semi-circular walk from Cockle Creek in the far south to Scotts Peak.

The Cradle Mountain-Lake St Clair park, the State's most popular and best-known, includes the 85km Overland Track from Cradle Valley to Lake St Clair, a walk past highland tarns and lakes, streams and waterfalls and mountain peaks, including Tasmania's highest mountain, Mount Ossa.

The Franklin-Gordon Wild Rivers National Park includes the Franklin River, the broad lower reaches of the Gordon and Frenchmans Cap, a mountain of white quartzite, with a sheer cliff face of 300 metres.

In 1997 the Valley of the Giants forest of Beech Creek and the Counsel River near Wayatinah were included in the Wild Rivers National Park, the latest in a series of significant forests to be permanently protected under Tasmania's conservation regime.

Tasmania's land mass covers 6.8 million hectares. Before European settlement, forests covered 4.8 million hectares. Clearing for the first farms saw that cover considerably reduced. Today forests still cover about 3.2 million hectares, 47 per cent of the land. Of that forest, 40 per cent is either protected in reserves, national parks or the World Heritage Area or is unavailable for logging.

The debate over the level of protection of Tasmania's forests pre-dates the other great environmental battles here in the 20th century, namely Lake Pedder and the Franklin River.

There is genuine environmental sensitivity about the use of forests, logging of old-growth trees, the conversion of native forest to plantations and the aesthetics of clearfelling. There is also a political paradigm. Tasmania's Hare-Clark system of proportional representation in the state House of Assembly and a similar electoral system for the Senate facilitate the election of minority party candidates and independents. Therefore, conservation has a political voice in Tasmania and the Greens have twice held the balance of power in the Assembly.

The counter view from industry is that Tasmania's forests are in safe hands, citing world's best practice in management as well as conservation, that the Government and the Parliament control an already responsible industry.

Central to the debate over forestry is the practice of clearfelling, burning and sowing wet eucalypt forests as a harvesting and regeneration tool.

In the natural cycle, the role of fire in regenerating wet eucalypt forests is established. Without wildfires, eucalypts dominate the rainforest understorey for their life span of about 400 years before falling to the forest floor and allowing the rainforest species – leatherwood, sassafras, celery-top pine and myrtle – to take over.

When an intense wildfire occurs, the forest floor is incinerated, providing a virtually sterile seed bed for the dormant eucalypt seeds in the soil to germinate, regenerating the eucalypt forest lost in the fire. The eucalypts grow faster than the rainforest seedlings and dominate the new forest.

In his book The Private Life of Plants: A Natural History of Plant Behaviour, Sir David Attenborough explains why the dominant species in Tasmania's wet eucalypt forests, the swamp gum or mountain ash (Eucalyptus regnans) cannot survive without fire.

"The threat to the survival of the spectacular forests of noble mountain ash is not, in fact, fire. It is the absence of fire," he says.

"If the great trees die from old age before flames have cleared the ground for their seedlings, then they will leave no successors.

"Paradoxically, such a forest will not survive unless much of it is first destroyed."

For many, this still does not justify Man's interference in the natural order of things in the forest. The political pressure on Tasmania's old-growth forests is intensifying, not abating.

It is only in relatively recent times that Tasmanians have emerged from their insular remoteness.

In many ways they felt they had been Third World members of a second-world society, isolated physically and psychologically from their countrymen on "the mainland".

This sense of isolation in Tasmania derives of course from the beginnings of the colony, when Van Diemen's Land was established as a penal settlement. From that time, came a sense of independence and the need for self-sufficiency, also a conservatism and adherence to traditional values.

Still today, Tasmanians are characterised by a simplicity, a lack of pretence and sophistication.

Twenty years ago when Lord Snowdon photographed Tasmania and its people he caused a storm. He captured an unsophisticated people, relics of the 50s. Snowdon's lens portrayed our people as faintly ridiculous.

The then premier Bill Neilson ranted that Snowdon had portrayed Tasmania as a second-rate Tierra del Fuego.

Today Snowdon would find a different race and a different place – people who are self-assured and content, content in the knowledge that they live, not in one of Earth's backwaters, but one of Earth's special places, a wild, natural island.

Swallows Nest Lakes at Mt La Perouse and Pindars Peak. La Perouse owes much of its attraction to its Permian sediments, the intrusion of resistant Jurassic dolerite and a modern glacial history so characteristic of Tasmanian highlands. The top of La Perouse consists of Triassic sediments.

King Billy pine (Athrotaxis selaginoides) *with deciduous beech* (Nothofagus gunnii), *Australia's only cold-weather, deciduous tree*

One of the sources of the D'Entrecasteaux River

Alpine cushion plant on Maxwell Ridge

Granite Beach, south coast

Maatsuyker islands

Dunes at Prion Bay

Needle Rocks off the south-west of Maatsuyker Island

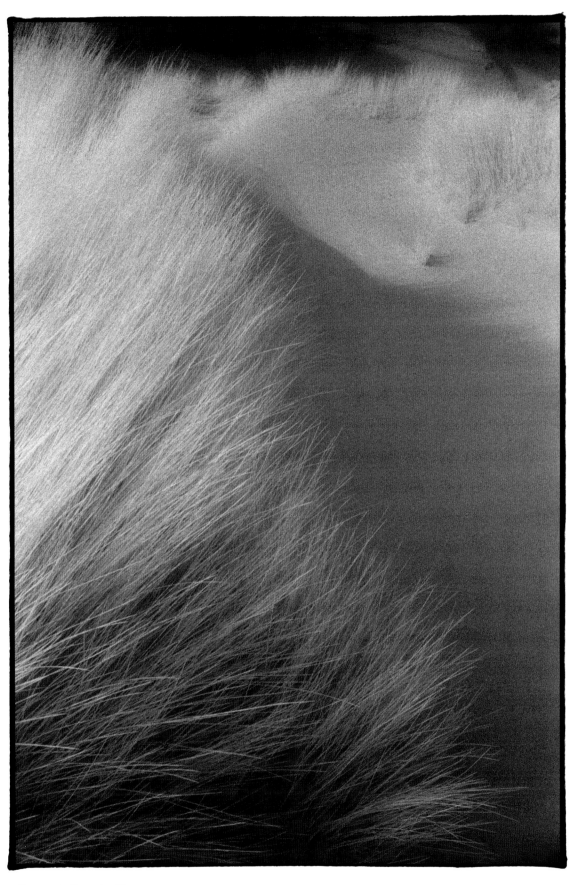

Dunes at Surprise Bay

Cox Bight beach

Point Eric protruding into Cox Bight

The creek at New Harbour

Hidden Bay

Ketchem Bay

Ketchem Island

Bathurst Harbour from Mt Rugby

Bathurst Harbour

Bathurst Channel at the foot of Mt Rugby

Horseshoe Inlet, Bathurst Harbour

Davey River

Davey River Gorge

West coast near Towterer Creek

Wedge-tailed eagle (Aquila audax)

An inquisitive juvenile wedge-tailed eagle (Aquila audax) on the wing in the De Witt Range near Towterer Creek

Frankland Range with the waters of Lake Pedder beyond

Opposite: Wreck Bay, north of Port Davey, takes its name from the wreck of the Norwegian barque Svenor, a three-masted, iron-hulled ship that was abandoned on Tasmania's west coast in 1914. Svenor sailed in ballast from Fremantle on 15 April 1914 bound for Newcastle, NSW. Two weeks out, the ballast shifted during a storm and Svenor began to list heavily. The crew cut away the rigging and part of the masts to prevent a capsize. She drifted eastwards for 24 days before closing on the Tasmanian west coast on 24 May. The crew abandoned her but the steamship Wainui, on its regular run from Melbourne to Strahan, arrived on the scene and a joint effort was made to take Svenor in tow. Heavy weather foiled the attempt. Svenor was set ablaze and abandoned in the expectation that she would sink. Six months later a team of track cutters found the hulk in the bay now known as Wreck Bay. She was later stripped of all salvageable equipment and left to rust away.

Pedder flumes, a feature of the quartzite beach at the original Lake Pedder

The new Lake Pedder. Frankland Range in the background

Lake Oberon in the Western Arthurs, south of Lake Pedder

These contorted rocks near Lake Oberon, now quartzite, were once thick sand deposited in a shallow sea, possibly 1100-1200 million years ago. They are the foundation rocks of south-west Tasmania's World Heritage Area.

Haven Lake in the Western Arthurs

A light display between weather fronts during a winter traverse of the Western Arthurs. These mountains are among the first struck by the westerly storms that sweep across the Southern Ocean to Tasmania in the latitudes known as the Roaring Forties.

The Boiler Plates, Eastern Arthur Range

Federation Peak, at the southern end of the Eastern Arthurs, is probably Tasmania's most sought-after mountain to climb. A Geelong

Grammar School party led by John Bechervaise was the first to climb the mountain in January 1949.

South-west Tasmania is subject to violent storms at any time of the year. Walkers who venture into these regions should be fit, experienced and suitably equipped for cold, wet and icy conditions.

Federation Peak with the Western Arthurs beyond

Federation Peak and Lake Geeves, named after Osborne Geeves, one of the pioneering family after whom the town of Geeveston is named.

They cut the first track from Geeveston to the Hartz Mountains and later extended it to the bottom of Federation Peak.

From Schnells Ridge, buttongrass-covered ranges against the serrated skyline of the Western Arthurs

Pink quartzite on glacial moraines with Lake Judd, Mt Eliza and Mt Sarah Jane in the background

Lakes below Mt Eliza and Mt Sarah Jane, near Mt Anne

Mt Anne

Old-growth swamp gums (Eucalyptus regnans) in the Andromeda Reserve, Styx Valley

Big Tree Reserve, Styx Valley

Styx River

Eucalyptus regnans in the lower Florentine. The world's tallest flowering plant grows up to 100 metres and lives for 400 years.

A stringy-bark (Eucalyptus obliqua) in the Lady Binney Reserve, Florentine Valley

Eucalyptus regnans stand, Manning Road Reserve, Florentine Valley

Beech-Counsel Valley of the Giants. Tall forests in the Beech Creek and Counsel River are part of the Franklin-Gordon Wild Rivers National Park.

Sassafras (Atherosperma moschatum) rainforest understorey emerging in the Beech-Counsel Valley of the Giants as the

dominant eucalypts mature

Rainforest fringing the Franklin River near Angel Rain Cavern

Descension Gorge

Irenabyss

Eucalypts at Tahune Creek near Irenabyss

Serenity Sound

Anaesthesia Ravine, Franklin River

The Log Jam

Gordon River

Frenchmans Cap

A westerly gale blasts Ocean Beach, Strahan

Buttongrass plains near Birchs Inlet. Western Tasmania is subject to heavy rainfall. Creeks and rivers rise quickly.

Blackwoods (Acacia melanoxylon) on the banks of the Pieman River at Corinna

Water from the World Heritage Area spills over the Reece Dam on the Pieman River

Pieman River at Corinna

Couta Rocks, north of Temma

The wreck of the schooner Alert about 5km south of the mouth of the Arthur River. She beached in a gale in March 1854. The crew, who all survived, walked overland to Mount Cameron and Woolnorth, where they were taken to Circular Head in two boats. The wreck re-emerged from the sand in 2003.

Lake Parangana on the Mersey River

Flowering wattle

Lake Rowallan

Tarns at Herods Gate, Walls of Jerusalem National Park

The Walls of Jerusalem

Solomons Throne

Pencil pines (Athrotaxis cupressoides), Walls of Jerusalem

Pencil pines, near Mt Jerusalem

Dixons Kingdom Hut, near the base of Mt Jerusalem, was built by Reg Dixon in the 1930s. The hut is built from pencil pine logs dragged from the nearby forest.

Mt Geryon in the Cradle Mountain-Lake St Clair National Park

Above: Barn Bluff   Below: Cradle Mountain

Mt Pelion West, Cradle Mountain in the distance

Deciduous beech (Nothofagus gunnii) and King Billy pine (Athrotaxis selaginoides) at Crater Lake, Cradle Mountain

Dove Lake, Cradle Mountain

Marakoopa Cave, Mole Creek

Slightly acid water dissolved 500 million-year-old limestone to create the Mole Creek caves. River gravels washed into the caves and the limestone cemented them into place. At the same time, huge boulders, once the foundation of the river above, were exposed in the cave ceiling, making a very unusual feature.

Trousers Point, Flinders Island

Goose Island at the western approach to Franklin Sound, which lies between Flinders and Cape Barren islands in the Furneaux group. Convicts built the Goose Island lighthouse in 1846.

Shallow lagoons on the east coast of Flinders Island host a variety of birdlife

Bay of Fires

Policemans Point near Ansons Bay

Bay of Fires

Scree fields on Ben Lomond, Tasmania's second-highest mountain

Alpine tarns frozen by morning frost

One of the White Knights (Eucalyptus viminalis) at the Evercreech Forest Reserve in the Fingal Valley, the tallest white gums in the world

The Tasmanian tree fern (Dixonia antarctica), a relic of the age when Tasmania and Antarctica were part of the supercontinent Gondwana

The Hazards, Freycinet peninsula

Wineglass Bay beach

Wineglass Bay and The Hazards

Great Oyster Bay, east coast

Beach at Schouten Island

Opposite: The crags of Freycinet peninsula and Maria Island National Park are home to the white-bellied sea eagle (Haliaeetus leucogaster). Sea eagles are not true eagles, which have feathered legs, but giant kites.

Lichen is a feature on the granite on the east coast of Schouten Island, south of Cape Forestier

The cleanest water in the world, Schouten Passage

Granite outcrops on Bear Hill, Schouten Island

Riedle Bay, Maria Island

Tasman Island

A weedy sea dragon (Phyllopteryx taeniolatus) in a giant kelp forest in Waterfall Bay, Tasman National Park

Dog Leg Cave, Waterfall Bay

The early French explorers described Cape Raoul as "an organ reposing on the surface of the sea". It is the best-known example of exposed dolerite columns, 170 million years old.

The Neck at Bruny Island

Lake Osborne and Devils Backbone, Hartz Mountains National Park

Multi-layered ice sheets on Lake Osborne

Wellington Range, behind Hobart

A streamside reserve at West Creek in the Arve Valley shows clearly the evolution of what happens in an undisturbed forest, in which the once dominant eucalypts give way to what had been the understorey of rainforest species.

Opposite: The life cycle of a forest in the Arve Valley. A tree that grew from a seed at the time that Abel Tasman discovered the island in 1642 collapses to the forest floor, decays and provides the seedbed for the next generation of the rainforest. Eucalypts in these wet forests require fire to remain the dominant species.

Huon River, in flood, from the Tahune AirWalk, looking towards Pear Hill and the confluence of the Picton and Huon rivers

Tahune stringy-bark

Huon River, Tahune

Opposite: A 400-year-old Huon pine (Lagarostrobus franklinii) in the Picton Valley. One of the longest-living organisms on Earth, it is a reminder of Tasmania's geological connections with Antarctica where fossil pollen almost identical with that of modern Huon pine has been found.

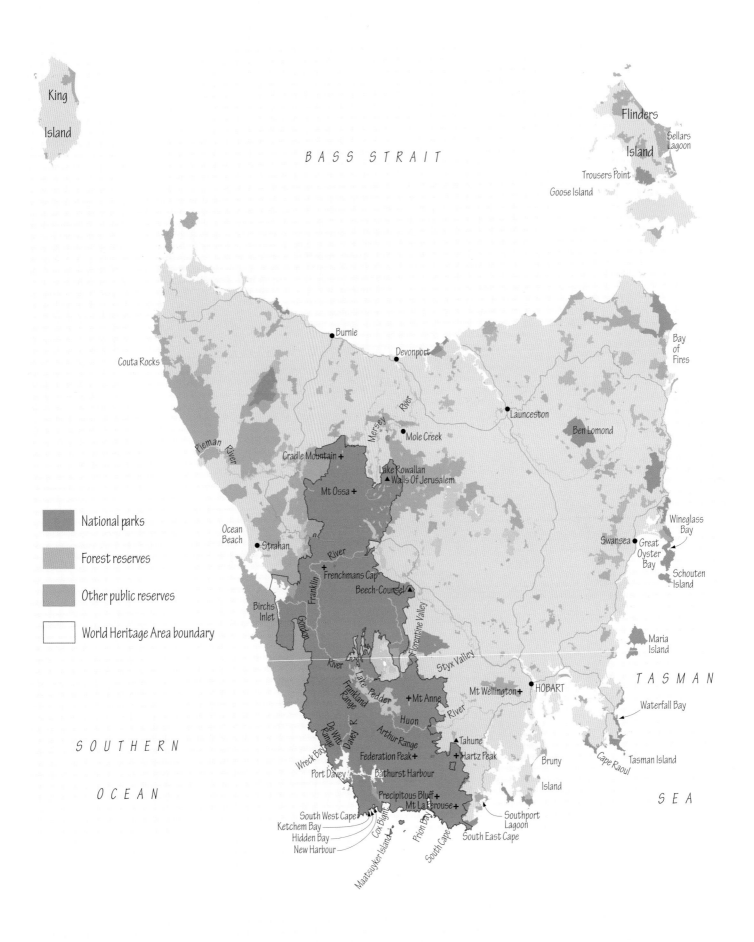

King
Island

BASS STRAIT

Flinders
Island
Sellars
Lagoon
Trousers Point
Goose Island

Couta Rocks

● Burnie

● Devonport

Bay
of
Fires

River

● Launceston

Mersey

● Mole Creek

Ben Lomond

Cradle Mountain +

Lake Rowallan
▲ Walls Of Jerusalem

Mt Ossa +

Pieman River

National parks

Forest reserves

Other public reserves

World Heritage Area boundary

Ocean
Beach

● Strahan

River

Frenchmans Cap +

Wineglass
Bay

Swansea ●
Great
Oyster
Bay

Beech-Cournel ▲

Schouten
Island

Birchs
Inlet

Franklin

Florentine Valley

Gordon

Maria
Island

River

Styx Valley

TASMAN

Lake Pedder

Frankland Range

Mt Anne +

River

Mt Wellington + ● HOBART

Waterfall Bay

Huon

De Witt Range

Davey R.

Arthur Range

▲ Tahune

Federation Peak +

+ Hartz Peak

Bruny

SEA

Cape Raoul

Tasman Island

Wreck Bay

Port Davey

Bathurst Harbour

Island

SOUTHERN

Precipitous Bluff +

Mt La Perouse +

Southport
Lagoon

OCEAN

South West Cape
Ketchem Bay
Hidden Bay
New Harbour

Cox Bight

Maatsuyker Island

Prion Bay

South Cape

South East Cape

Map by Peter Boyer using data © 2004 Tasmap

Approximately 40 per cent of Tasmania is protected in World Heritage Area, national parks, forest and other reserves.

ACKNOWLEDGEMENTS

Richard Bennett acknowledges the cooperation and assistance of the following people and organisations:
Premier Paul Lennon
Forests and Forest Industry Council – Trevor Bird
Sir Guy Green for the foreword
Bruce Montgomery and Professor Pat Quilty for the text
Vicki Montgomery for editing
Pauline de Vos for the design
Alice Bennett for creative input
Ben Britten for scanning at Photolith
Peter Boyer and Tasmap for the map
Paul Courto and Ian Rosevear – Printing Authority of Tasmania

For companionship in the bush or at sea: Stuart Mc Gregor, the late David Ripper,
John Frankcomb, Graham Carter, Jon Grunseth, Peter Shield, Barry Palmer, Christopher Burton, Gordon Bishop, John Gray, Peter and Claire Marmion,
Luuk Veltkamp, Dr Joe Cannon and my family

Mark Holdsworth and Dave James – Orange-bellied parrot recovery programme
Tasair pilots Matthew Bester, Brian Clifford, John Pugh, John Townley, Ralph Schwertner and the late Nick Tanner
Par Avion Wilderness Tours – Greg Wells
Rotor-Lift Helicopters – pilot Peter Elliott
Helicopter Resources – pilot Leigh Hornsby
Freycinet Sea Charters – Duncan Sinclair
Forestry Tasmania – Evan Rolley and Graham Sargison
Eaglehawk Dive Centre – Gary Myors and Karen Gowlet-Holmes
Rafting Tasmania – Graham Mitchell and Tim Trevaskis
Canon Australia Pty Limited –Alan Brightman
Fujifilm – Kevin Cooper
West Coast Yacht Charters – Trevor and Megs Norton
Tahune AirWalk
Mole Creek Caves
Max Stephenson

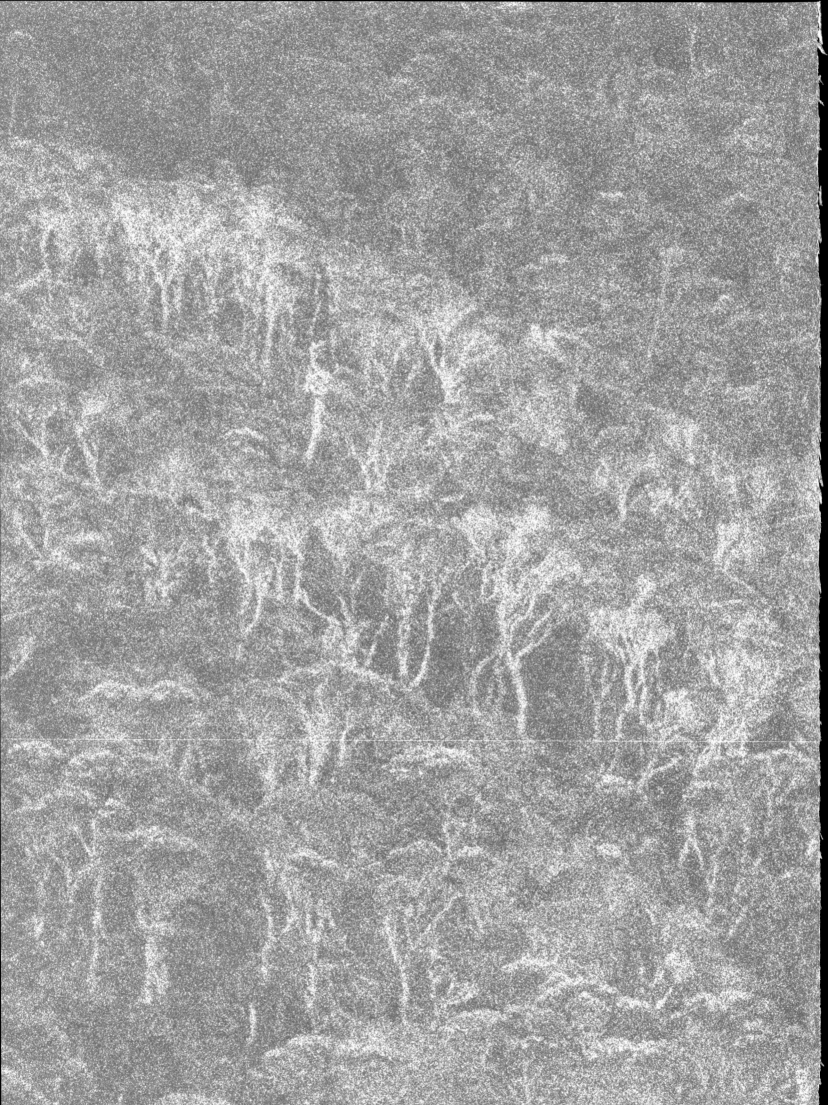